# 7x7+7

## Ray Ed...

GW00707308

FOR JUDITH

It matters not
The length of the message,
Nor even
The statue of the medium;
A loving connection
With those gone before —
Such a joy
Amongst life's tedium.

1

# SEVEN BY SEVEN PLUS SEVEN

Published by R A Associates
Printed in the UK

## Dedications

With sincere thanks and love to those
without whom this book would not have
been possible :-
Robert and Judy Lebesque and all members
of the Lyndhurst Circle, past and present,
whose support and love always encouraged
me, despite my sense of humour.
Melanie Pollie, without the Family Gathering
courses my calling may not have emerged
when it did.
My partner Sam, whose love and support has
kept me going on my verses and made my life
truly magical.
My Spirit inspirers who work so hard to bring
me the verses. I hope they don't get too cross
when I fail to get one down, or am tempted to
tamper with their originals!

## CONTENTS

## The Story so Far

In October 2005 I was fortunate enough to be invited to join the Lyndhurst Development Circle led by Robert Lebesque. I was very nervous and unsure of why I was there. The friendly and supportive environment at the circle gradually led me to relax and relate to the world of Spirit in ways I might not have found elsewhere.

In February 2006, as a result of encouragement from friends at Circle, I enrolled to go on the Family Gathering III spiritual development course at Cober Hill near Scarborough. Whilst sitting in one of the morning meditations led by Melanie, I found that I was being inspired to write verse. It was brought into my mind at quite a fast rate, and the verse "God's Ministers" was written. I read it out to the assembled friends at the Gathering, and it was very popular. More verses came during the rest of that course and I wrote them in my journal, my constant companion.

After my return from FGIII, I started to find that verses kept coming into my mind at all sorts of different times, and on all sorts of different topics. I started to use a small digital voice recorder to get them down, so that I didn't lose them. I typed them up as fast as I could to try and keep pace with the inspiration.

Over the last year, I have found that I get something most days, even if only a part verse, or a topic to be developed as a verse. Some days I will receive up to 6 in a day. If this happens every day for a week, I have trouble keeping up! I now have over 300 completed verses and over 500 works in progress.

Having read some of my verses to others, I have been encouraged to get them into print in order to be able to share them with others. This also seems to be what my inspirers want, and who am I to argue? I believe this is the first in a series of books I will bring together and look forward to working on future ones.

It would be remiss of me not to mention the help of Robert Goodwin, my printer and publisher, whose details were given to me at Family Gathering IV this year, and without whose help this book would not exist.

I hope you enjoy reading them as much as I enjoy bringing them through. Watch out for Percillus - one of my favourites!

7 x 7 + 7

# FATHERHOOD OF GOD

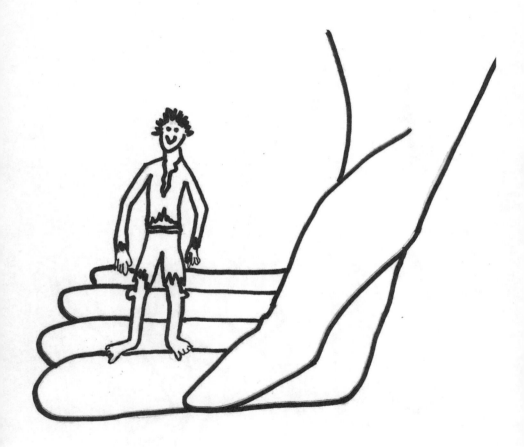

# FATHERHOOD OF GOD

If all my clothes
Were hand me downs,
And my feet
Remained unshod,
Still no one
Could remove
From me
The Fatherhood of God.

No other can
Deny my place,
In this
Akashic Game;
And keep me from
The knowledge
Of the source,
From whence I came.

My soul has chose
To come here,
Feeling joyousness
And pain;
A chance to earn
Some brownie points,
For when
I'm back again.

Alone inside
My overcoat,
With just me
On my tod;
I feel
My spirit's
Closeness to
The Fatherhood of God.

Ssshh...

Ssshh...

## QUIET DIGNITY

There is a quiet dignity
Within the heart of man;
Where moral strength
And courage
Reflect God's masterplan.

Where those of less ability
Are judged not by their lack;
And those returning 'cos they've failed
Receive
A welcome back.

Where all are classed as equals,
Without colour, race or creed;
And each receives their measure,
Based on fairness,
Not on greed.

Alternate views are welcome,
With no need to make a change;
Where just because of difference
We won't
Be labelled strange.

Where genders stand together,
And the children have their say;
Not pressured into adulthood
While they still
Need to play.

With fresh ideas invited,
As a chance for all to see;
How inspiration
Generates
A strong diversity.

All petty minor differences
Are calmly set aside;
No need for one to walk in fear,
By others
Terrified.

So reach up to the universe,
And feel the cosmic tug;
And know God's love of dignity
Makes equals
In a hug.

Where humour's situational,
The province of the clown;
Not based on use of swear-words,
Or on putting
Others down.

There is a quiet dignity
Within the heart of man;
Which comes from
God's intention,
Before the Earth began.

## WHENCE DO I COME

Whence do I come?
And whither I go?
Tis held in the essence,
The source and the flow.


The purpose, the reason,
For my being here
Is writ by the hand
Of the Great Gazetteer.


The mission, the style,
The course I've begun
A bipedic roadmap,
My Akashic Fun Run!

## LIFE

Life is what happens
When you're making plans;
Be there with the leaders,
Not with "also rans".

Some think just one shot
Is all that you get;
So friend do not waste it
By frivolous fret.

Some think you come back,
Time and again;
Reincarnated
To learn from the pain.

Some think there's nothing
That waits at the end;
A nothing filled blackness,
So enjoy time you spend.

Some think we progress,
From low to the high;
If we learn the lessons
We're shown from on high.

Some think we all are
Just part of one whole;
A tiny extraction
Of the One Cosmic Soul.

Some think we're sinners,
With suffering to bear;
The more pain we have here
Will show God we care.

Life is what happens,
While God watches all;
Let us not waste it,
Let Him see it's a Ball!

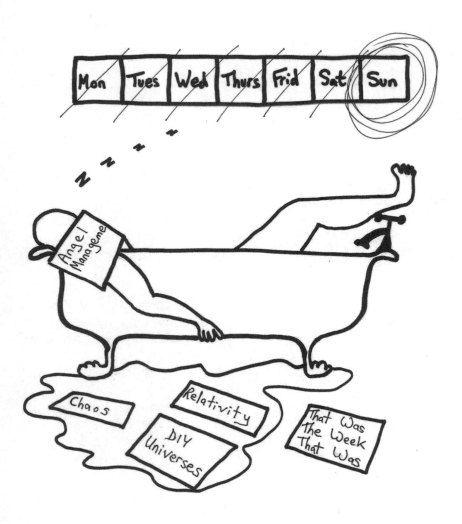

## MY GOD HAS

My God has
Got His hands full,
With Creation aftermath
The long days
In eternity,
Defined by lack of staff.

How quick we are
To judge Him when,
He seems us to ignore;
He must see
We're important, when
We're knocking on His door?

The Big Bang
Was a great idea,
To spread Himself around;
With consequential
Substance,
Light and vision, moving sound.

Compassionate,
I'm sure He is,
For all created souls;
But He does have
Other irons,
Heating in the cosmic coals.

With angels
There to help Him,
He can delegate some parts
But not creating
Human souls,
Or what goes in their hearts.

So like most
Earthly fathers,
God is busy every day;
He sets our lives
In motion,
Then He lets us run and play.

His mind works
In dimensions
That we cannot contemplate
Ten thousand,
Million universes
Growing at a different rate.

My God has
Got His hands full,
With Creation aftermath;
Saturdays are
His busiest,
On Sundays, time for bath!

## CHASING GOD

I've chased my God,
Both far and wide;
Wishing that
He didn't hide:
This way,
That way,
In a tizz;
Wondering just
Where my God is.

I looked for God,
Up hill, down vale;
In places bright,
In place pale:
Inside,
Outside,
Upstairs, down;
In the country,
In the town.

I've sought my God,
With much ado;
In churches old,
And churches new:
Chaplains,
Ministers,
Vicars too;
Have given me
Their point of view.

I've heard of God,
In wooden pews;
With lots of don'ts,
And too few do's:
Sinning,
Spinning,
Bibles thumped;
My view of God
Always gazumped.

I've talked to God,
And called His name;
Was He Him?
Or really Dame?
Abiding,
Chiding,
Big and small;
Was He really
There at all?

I've challenged God,
With act and thought;
Asked did good deeds
Count for nought?
Praying,
Straying,
On the run;
Live with fear,
Or live for fun?

I've cursed my God,
When times were hard;
Bits that left me
Bruised and scarred;
Seeking,
Shrieking,
Answers to;
The point of what
I'm living through.


I found my God,
When chasing stopped;
When out of energy,
Down I flopped:
Disarming,
Charming,
Mystified;
He's always with me,
There inside!

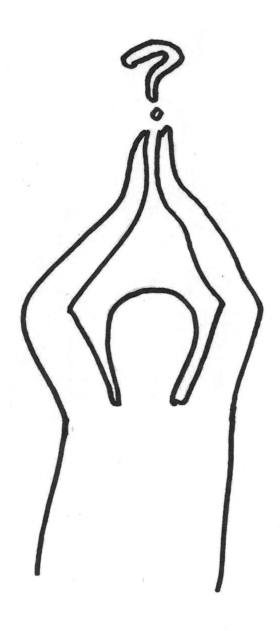

## WHO IS IT

Who is it
That I turn to,
When I need
A little prod;
When I get stuck,
In Earthly things,
Neglecting
Father God?

When I am
Lost and lonely,
And the world
Has put me down;
And everything
I step in
Is an evil
Smelling brown.

When I feel
I'm at the bottom,
And don't know
Which way's up;
Half full, maybe,
Half empty;
I can't even
Find the cup!

I only have
To raise my voice,
And say a
Prayer or two;
And draw divine
Attention
To the things
I'm going through.

Knowing that
My God is there,
To harken
To my voice;
Even if
His words to me
Are that - "I"
Made this choice!

This world is
All embracing,
All consuming,
In its ways;
But I should
Still remember,
That in Spirit
My soul stays.

The Father has
This give to me,
A chance to
See His works;
Emotions,
Things, experience
Some smoothly,
Some in jerks.

So I am wrong
To criticise,
Bemoaning
So my fate;
I know that,
In the Spirit world,
My God  and
Loved ones wait.

7 x 7 + 7

# BROTHERHOOD OF MAN

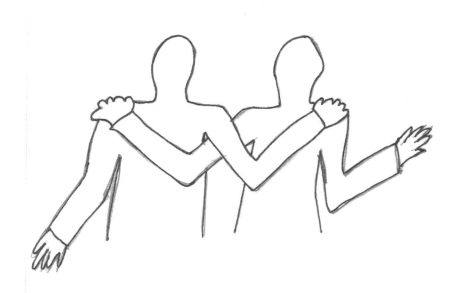

## AGE OF INNOCENCE

Where went the age of innocence
When childhood was for play?
When children didn't have to think
What grade they'd be today.

Where war itself was enemy,
We'd won the right to be
Hopeful for a better life,
And always to be free.

With dustbins full of potters clay,
And pots of powder paint,
And teachers gave a cuddle
If a child was feeling faint.

Our land was fit for heroes,
With a pension there to see,
That soldiers living to old age
Could live independently.

With development of talent
More important than exams;
And turning out good citizens,
Not a measure weighed in grams.

Our health scheme was the envy
Of great nations far and wide;
With nurses, doctors, dentists,
There for all and qualified.

Where differences between us
Showed a strong society;
With things that I could do for you,
And things you'd do for me.

Where went the happy quiet days,
Before the mobile phone?
Without the irritation
Of that ever ringing tone?

Where manners and behaviour
Were a mark of true respect;
And foul mouthed, loud aggression
Hadn't all those lives yet wrecked.

Where went the simple furnishing,
That made a comfy home?
Before the must have adverts,
Which see all our money blown?

Where politicians spoke of truth,
And led responsibly;
Resigning if a scandal showed
They'd lied to you and me.

The streets were safe for walking,
By the young and old alike;
And not a place to fear attack,
For wallet, life or bike.

Where work was there a-plenty,
With rewards for working hard;
And showing love for others
Didn't seem a joker card.


Where younger folk related
To the wisdom of the old;
Combining it with energy,
To build a future bold.


Where festival tradition,
And the customs of the past,
Gave us all a feeling
That stability would last.


I guess that age of innocence
For sure has blown away?
I wish that how I felt back then
Were how I feel today!

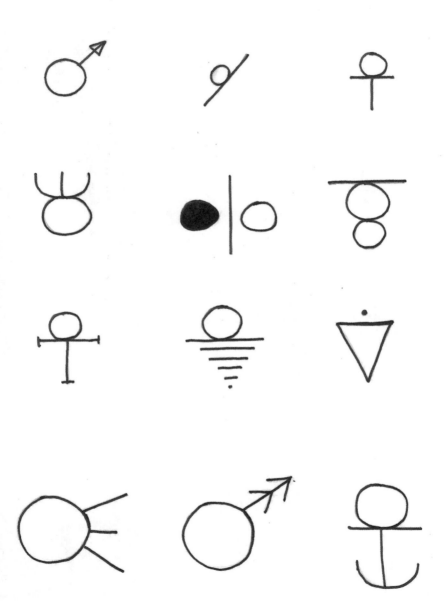

## DIFFERENT

Those who think
We're different,
Should look
And think again;
For we all
Are members
Of the
Brotherhood of Men.

And though they
May seek labels,
Which set
Some men apart;
Our source
Is fundamental,
It's the
Universal Heart.

In seeking out
The differences,
It's strange,
But very true;
The process
Makes them
More aware
Of likenesses in view.

So when
They find
That we
Diverge,
A hundred times or ten;
They really should
Just recognise
The Brotherhood of Men.

## ENERGY OF THE CIRCLE

The energy of the circle,
A going round vibration,
Is going round
And coming round
With loving contemplation.

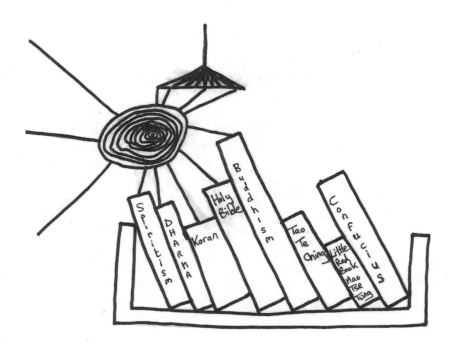

## ANNALS

The dust encrusted annals
Of religions
Of the world,
Say all the things
We could achieve
If fists were
All uncurled.

How many tons of guidance
Are recumbent
In our homes?
Theological
Subsidence
In these wondrous,
Mighty tomes.

If we distilled the messages
And themes
They all contain,
Our lives would be
More loving then,
And less concerned
With blame.

How many God's and prophet words
Exhort us
To make war?
How many teach us
To be rich,
And to ignore
The poor?

If we set aside our differences
And seek
How we're the same,
Then we could hold
Our heads heads up high,
And not be bowed
In shame.

So in the cause of wisdom,
Let us read
A book or two;
They're lying on
The bookshelf there,
Just awaiting
Me and you

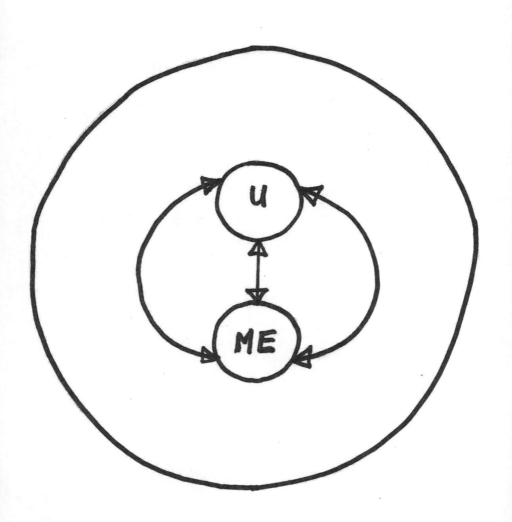

## HOW WOULD IT BE..

How would it be
If I were you,
And you were me
In turn?
We'd look inside
Each other's heads,
And see what we
Could learn.

How would it be
To feel like me,
And me to feel
Your cares?
I'd know your concerns,
And what passion burns;
Deep inside where
Prejudice flares.

How would it be
If we could both
Reach deep inside
Ourselves?
And find the source
Which is God, of course,
Whose books are on
Our shelves.

## I SEE WHERE

I see where
You're coming from,
And though
I don't agree;
You've every right
To be there,
Though you're
Different
To me.

I do not
Seek to change
Your world,
And make
You live in mine;
So let's respect
Each other's views,
'Cos opposites
Are fine.

## YOUR VIEWS

When the groundswell
Of opinion
Is the views
You hold
Are wrong;
It's time
For you to
Challenge
Why you hold
Those views so strong!

7 x 7 + 7

# COMMUNION OF SPIRITS AND

# MINISTRY OF ANGELS

## ANGEL DUST

Angel dust was falling,
In the land
Of Katmandu;
It fell in shades
Of pink 'n white,
Of blue and purple too.

The angels flew
From mountain tops,
To sprinkle forth their dust;
It carried
Special messages,
Of love and hope and trust.

It covered all the landscape,
In a wondrous,
Magic glow;
Good wishes from
The ones above,
To those of us below.

Any could partake of it,
And gain its
Special gift;
But it only works
For those of us
Who find it in a drift.

And so if you should
Find yourself
Adrift in Katmandu;
Be sure you have
Your brush and pan,
To make a drift come true.

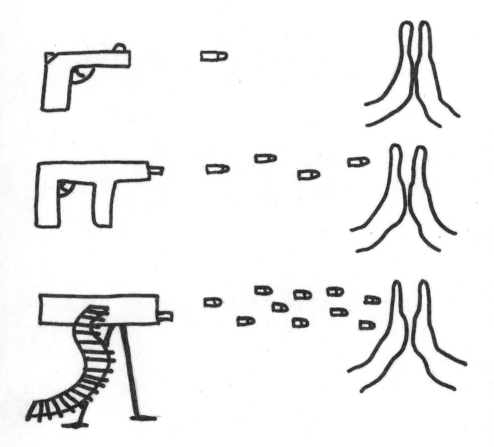

## BULLETS

For every bullet
That's been shot,
An angel says a prayer;
To counter
All the anger and
The hatred and despair.


For every unkind
Thought and word,
The Spirits seek to find;
Ways to bring
The light of love
Into the human mind.


For every nasty
Selfish deed,
That's wrought on anyone;
The fairies cast
A spell of charm,
Those things to overcome.


For every person
In the world,
Choice is theirs to make;
So save your bullets,
Deeds and words,
Hold back for others' sake.

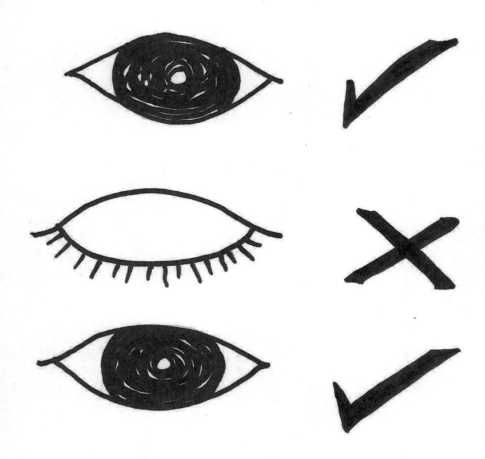

## DON'T BLINK

Don't blink,
And miss the link,
With Spirits
From upstairs;
The Spirit panel
Will use your channel,
With thoughts
Quite unawares.
So don't dismiss
That angel kiss,
So gentle
On your brow;
Accept the gift,
And let it lift
The moods
Of here and now!

## GOD'S MINISTERS

There's many kinds of ministry,
When all is said and done;
There's ministry to millions
And ministry to one.

You may just be a channel,
So channel good and true;
The words may come from up above,
Or mixed with bits of you.

Just how to see your ministry,
And how to make it work?
To stand and talk to hundreds,
Or just a private quirk?

You may perform on platform,
In circle you may sit;
But wher'er it is you join in,
You're sure to do your bit.

There's ministries to spread the word,
And those of evidence;
But there is no ministry
For sitting on the fence.

And do not look to judges,
No critics let you sway;
If you are working truly,
The Spirits have their say.

So reach up to the cosmic,
And see what you can get;
There's many ways to minister,
There's nothing fixed and set.

You may give words aplenty,
Or you may just give a few;
You may just get a picture,
Or a smell may just come through.

And if you seek sincerely,
And with an open heart;
The Spirit world will help you,
And show you how to start.

But what you get has travelled
A long way to get here;
So speak out loud and clearly,
So the audience can hear.

You may not feel you got much,
You may just get a bit;
But to someone waiting out there
It may make a perfect fit.


So do not be fainthearted,
Just give it all as got;
Let Spirit be the judges,
Of how you keep the plot.


And always please remember,
That nothing goes to waste;
So do not try to rush it,
There is no need for haste.


Philosophy inspires us,
And messages are proof;
Just let the Spirits work through you,
Don't try to be aloof.


When you make your connection,
Enjoy it, have some fun;
When you minister to millions,
Or you minister to one.

BAD RECEPTION ZONE

## LOSS

If I listen not
To Spirit,
Then they'll listen not
To me;
And what a loss
To both of us
That will turn out
To be.

## SITTING HERE

Sitting here,
Receptive,
In a Spirit
State of mind;
Sending thoughts
To them upstairs,
I am
Their way inclined.

Linking with
Eternity,
No thought
Of selfish gain;
Just simple minded
Channelling,
My mind
A Spirit train.

I seek to make
Connection,
To the Spirit
World above;
And see how
I can serve them,
I am
Offering my love.

Bringing through
A loved one,
From that grand
Eternal realm;
My mind a
Floating tiller,
With a
Spirit at the helm.

And love provides
The channel,
For a Spirit
To come through;
Circled by
Protection,
So no harm
Can come to you.

Loving centred
Energy,
To guide my
Time on Earth;
Acting as
A medium
Will give
My life more worth.

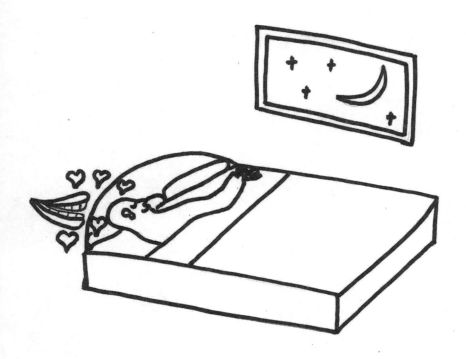

## WHISPERS IN THE NIGHT

I whisper
Words
Beside you,
In the quiet
Of the night;
I whisper
Words
Of loving,
But you do not
Hear it right.


I whisper
'Cos I'm
Close to you,
You know
When I am near;
I whisper
Words of loving,
So they
Linger
In your ear.


I whisper
'Cos I
Love you,
And I wish
To let you know
You're thought of
As you travel,
On the
Earth Plane,
There below.

7 x 7 + 7

# CONTINUOUS EXISTENCE

# OF THE HUMAN SOUL

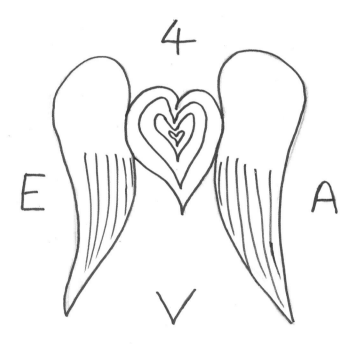

## THAT LIFE FOREVER....

That life forever,
Never land
Is just a blink away;
It makes you think
We're on the brink,
Whilst on the Earth we play!

That warm embrace,
That happy face,
Are riches more than wealth;
For love rewards,
And conquers swords,
And love should need no stealth!

That wish you well
Third parallel,
Exists in space around;
And if we link,
With loving pink,
Our dear ones can be found!

That softest touch,
It means so much,
A brush upon your face;
A Spirit sign,
A force benign,
Within your loving space!

That feather found,
Is love around,
With angel caring wings;
So tarry not
On what you've got,
There is no point in things!

That loving laugh,
That happy path,
Will lead us through each test;
And when we go,
We're sure to know,
That we have done our best!

## THE GATEWAY

The gateway,
That's before us,
On the journeys
Of the soul;
Is there to
Bid us enter,
To the place
Where we'll be whole.

# BEYOND THE DEEP

Beyond the deep,
Beyond the calm,
Beyond the swaying, silver palm;
Beyond the wind,
Beyond the rain,
Beyond the laughter and the pain;
Beyond it all,
Beyond it then,
Existence can begin again.

## SANCTITY OF SPIRIT

The sanctity
Of Spirit,
This earthly life
Can't harm;
And though
You seem insensitive,
Your essence
Keeps it's charm.

Reaching for
Your destiny,
Can make
Your life fulfilled;
Living life,
Just selfishly,
Will see
Your essence spilled.

Reaching down,
Inside yourself,
You'll find
The best of you;
That jewel-encrusted
Centre,
So often
Hid from view.

Your brain
Can be a dustbin,
For the clutter
Of your life;
So set about
Recycling,
And wield
The surgeon's knife.

Keep your eyes
On victory,
And all
Will be revealed;
Use your link
To Spirit,
From whom nothing
Is concealed.

Cut away
Excesses,
Let your flotsam
Drift away;
Keep your
Colours well defined,
Avoid
The shades of grey.

Keep what's
Really useful,
Letting go
Of all the rest;
Keeping hold
Of quality,
To reach
For what is best.

Going back
To Spirit,
You will leave
Your goods behind;
So keep
Sanctity of Spirit
Ever present
In your mind.

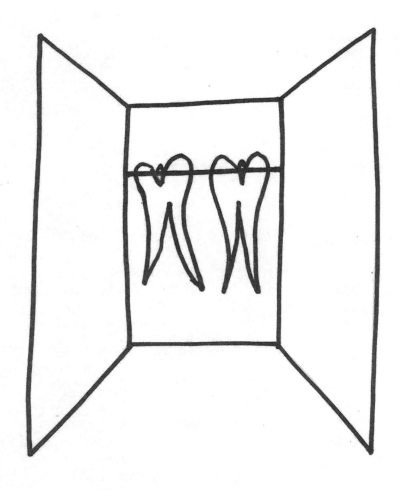

# YOUR ANGEL WINGS

Your angel wings
Are waiting,
In a cupboard,
Just upstairs;
They're ready if
Your exit's smooth,
Or takes you
Unawares.
The size of them
Might vary,
To reflect
Your earthbound score;
But angel wings
Are waiting,
In a cupboard,
By Heaven's door.

Miles of Smiles

## GO

Go with love,
Go with cheer,
Go without any tear;
For the love
That I give you
Is always right here.

Go with love,
Go with light,
Go without any spite;
For the love
That I give you
Is there day and night.

Go with fun,
Go with joy,
That no man can destroy;
For the love
That I bring you
Is for you to enjoy.

Go with song,
Go with glee,
Go with memories of me;
For the love
That I bring you
Is sweet melody.

Go with speed,
Go with pace,
And a smile on your face;
For the love
That I give you
Is a lifetime embrace.

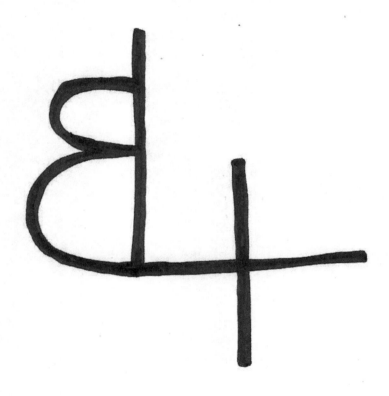

## BEFORE

Sometimes
A fleeting memory,
Of things we were before,
Reminds us
That our souls have had
More lifetimes
To explore.

The essence
Of a former path,
That we have freely trod,
Reminds us
There are many ways
To celebrate
Our God.

These many days,
And many ways,
Have taught us many things;
Including pain
We can't explain,
And joys that
Loving brings.

The strive to gain,
Our use of brain,
And faith in angel wings;
The cosmic rhythm
In our soul,
An inner song
That sings.

The beauty of
The sunlight,
And the fear of darkest night;
The raucous
Laugh of happiness,
And joyous eyes
So bright.

The chance to
See a million things,
And hear their stories told;
The chance to
Live in comfort,
Or in misery
Untold.

The starkest
Life of poverty,
Of starving in the cold;
Or one lived
Out in luxury,
All shimmering
In gold.

Whichever path
We've trodden,
Wherever we have been;
With lives all trod
In filthiness,
Or footsteps
Trodden clean.

The many things
We've learned
Upon travels in the past;
The lessons hard,
And easier,
Expectations
All surpassed.

Before things,
Not forgotten,
Give foundation to our way;
The life we're living,
Here and now,
Before will
Pave the way.

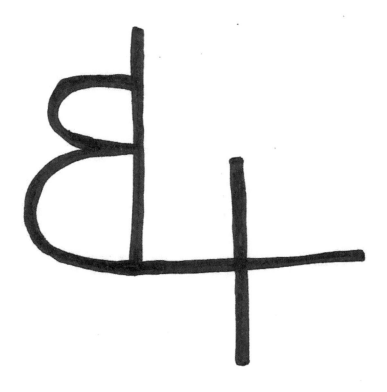

7 x 7 + 7

# PERSONAL RESPONSIBILITY

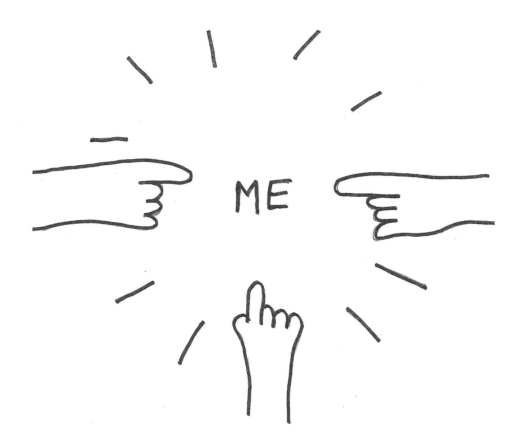

ME

## ABOVE THE NOISE

Above the noise,
Above the din,
I hear the
Still small voice within.

It speaks to me
Of things so wise,
And to my questions
Gives replies.

It counsels me
To heed my heart,
And let gut feelings
Play their part.

Its there to help,
And to advise;
Not to dictate,
Or compromise.

It seeks no power
Over me;
Nor wants to share
My entity.

Its there to give,
Without return;
As on my path
I try to learn.

Tots up no score,
And judges not;
It will be heard,
Won't be forgot.

However much
I justify,
The still small voice
Comes forth unshy.

If selfish motives
Fill my mind,
A conscience,
Suddenly I find.

If harming others
Has appeal,
The still small voice
Won't add its seal.

It makes me see
Another view,
Indifference
It does eschew.

Above the noise,
Above the din,
With that small voice
I might just win

## COCKIN A DEAF'UN

I can cock a deaf'un
With the best
That you can find;
Choosing not
To hear things
When I feel that way inclined.

Things that I'm not hearing
May be things
That I don't like;
Things that stop
My nice soft ride
And make me take a hike.

Things that put in front of me
The wrongs that
I have done;
Things that make me
See the clouds
Where I'd rather see the sun.

Things that cause discomfort,
In my mind
Or in my heart;
Things I knew
I shouldn't have
Right from the very start.

Things that challenge my beliefs
In just how
Good I am;
Things that do not
Praise me, but
Are more inclined to damn.

Things that I have left undone
Where action
Was required;
Mistakes I've made
Through clumsiness
Or just because I'm tired.

Things my conscience
Warned me of
But I ignored the sign;
Things I did
I knew were wrong,
Malicious, not benign.

Advice I should have followed,
Or a path
I should have took;
Petty little
Nuisance things,
Or where I've been a crook.

Though I don't want to hear them
With my motives
Yet to hide;
My conscience will
Remember them
And make me squirm inside.

And though I cock a deaf'un,
If my eyes
Are downward cast;
You'll know your words
Have found their mark,
And not gone shooting past.

# TRUE JOY OF LIVING

The true joy of living
I've only just found
Didn't cost me a million,
Didn't cost me a pound.

I didn't have to search
In a place far away;
Nor surf on the net
On some IT highway.

I didn't have to struggle
For hundreds of hours;
I didn't have to battle
The darkest of powers.

I didn't have to fight
With the demons inside;
I didn't have to run
And I didn't have to hide.

I didn't have to research
Through hundreds of books;
No searching in crannies,
No searching in nooks.

I sought out no wise man,
No sage or guru;
No scientist or boffin
Told me what to do.

No stars in the heaven,
Showed me the true way;
I didn't have to labour
By night and by day.

I cast me no rune stones,
Saw no psychic fella;
No counsellor helped me,
Saw no fortune teller.

I climbed me no mountain,
Nor swam any sea;
Explored no great jungle,
Paid no one a fee.

I went in no coal mine,
Explored not one cave;
I didn't have to show
I was both strong and brave.

I didn't have to sing out
With purest of voice;
I just had to see that
Each day I had choice.

My choice was so easy
To love life and see,
That if I loved others,
They'd also love me.

## TIDE OF TENDERNESS

Turn the tide of tenderness
Upon YOUR caring soul,
And let its waves of gentleness
Help make your being whole;
For what use all this tenderness,
If just on others spent?
When on yourself such viciousness
Is what you feel is meant?
If you believe that tenderness
Is what each soul should share,
With universal thoughtfulness
Please show YOURSELF you care;
If you believe that others
Are hurt by just a thought
Then why allow such injury
To your soul be self wrought?

SLOW DOWN

DIVERT

WAY CLOSED

NO ENTRY

ALTERNATE ROUTE

## DELAYS

Delays
Allow reflection
On the way
I lead my life;
A chance for
Introspection,
Rather than
A course for strife.

A chance to view
The methods,
And the systems
I employ;
A chance to take
Some time out,
From the stressful
Hoypolloy.

Why should I then
Get worked up,
When things aren't
What I expect?
They always
Have their reason
For a cosmic
Interject.

They may think
That I'm losing
The perspective
That I need;
When half my life's
So busy,
Spent in travelling
At speed.

Maybe they want
To whisper
Words of comfort
In my ear;
If they think
That I am losing it,
And that I
Need a steer.

Could they want
To be round me?
Slow me from
My normal rush?
Wanting to
Remind me
Of a certain
Kind of hush?

They may just
Want to prod me,
And remind me
That my world,
Is bigger than
The corner,
Where I'm usually
Safely curled.

For what price
All this tenderness,
And loving
There on tap;
If my soul
Is agitated,
Just reacting
To the strap?

They may want me
To work it out,
And not just
To be told;
To learn, then,
From experience;;
Reflections
When on hold.

Delays
Can break the pattern
Of the days,
Or months,
Or years;
Allowing fresh approaches,
Thus avoiding
Stubborn tears.

They may think
That I'm heading
Down a wrong track,
Road, or path;
Which possibly
Could lead me
To a cosmic,
Early bath.

I may think I know
What they think,
Or may really
Hear them say;
Whatever are
The facts of it,
I should welcome
Each delay.

## TAKE CHARGE

Sometimes in life
You must take charge,
And make yourself the boss;
Not leave it up to others,
Or with a coin make toss.


For others may not
Not see your worth,
And just put forth their own;
Rallying the company,
To leave you on your own.


By being boss
You can control,
The actions and the speed;
Dishing out with fairness,
Where another may use greed.


Being boss
You can affect,
The way that others view;
The quality of justice,
And the way that they see you.


So do not be
Fainthearted, when,
The need to lead stands out;
Being boss is sometimes
What your life is all about.

## DO YOU CARE

Do you care enough to be
The best that you can be?
Or will you feel
You wasted life,
When you reach eternity?

Will you whistle on the pathway,
As you walk towards the light?
Or curse the times
You didn't try,
Your brain cells to excite?

Will loving times with others
Be the stageposts of your path?
Will you wish you'd
Been less serious,
And more inclined to laugh?

Will you smile as you recall
The lovers that you've known?
Or wish you'd
Shared more cuddles,
In a life lived so alone?

Will you leave behind the riches,
Carefully gathered on this plane?
Will you take
Your good deeds with you,
As you go back home again?

Will the hills resound with echoes,
Of the souls who shared your time?
Will you clean up
All the mess you made,
And cause the bells to chime?

Do you care enough to be,
The best that you can be?
I hope that I
Audition well,
When I reach eternity!

7 x 7 + 7

# ETERNAL PROGRESS OPEN

# TO EVERY HUMAN SOUL

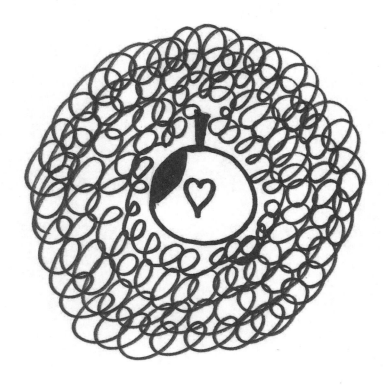

## LIFE WHEN WRAPPED

Life when wrapped
In cotton wool,
Is very safe, but boring;
If all your team
Is in defence,
You stand no chance of scoring.

If we complain
That we feel pain,
And we don't want the risk;
We'll never feel
That rush of blood,
When pace is set to brisk.

We settle in
Our comfort groove,
Our patterns make us sure;
But when life is
Predictable,
Excitement is no more.

We need to have
Respect for life,
Especially our own;
But if we don't
Extend ourselves,
We never will have grown.

Safe times, sure,
We need to have,
To gather up our strength;
But we should find
Life's quality,
And not just seek it's length

So throw away
The cotton wool,
Seek not the insulation;
Let life contain
Adventure times,
Intrinsic animation.

## WILL YOU

Will you
Seek out adventures,
In places untold?
Or stay by
Your fireside,
And never
Be cold?

Will you
Nourish your talents,
With vitality?
Or stay with
The wing clips,
And never
Be free?

Will you
Travel the wideworld,
And seek out it's charm?
Or stay in
A safe place,
And never
Know harm?

Will you
Wear angel wing-boots,
And walk in the sky?
Or stay under
Rainclouds,
And never
Be dry?

Will you
Seek soul excitement,
And let it run free?
Or act out
Survival,
With eyes
Just on me?

Will you
Ride on a dragon,
And fly through the mist?
Or stay in,
A loner,
And never
Be kissed?

Will you
Swim with the dolphins,
And dance on the surf?
Or count up
Your pennies,
To see
What you're worth?

Will you
Seek out adventures,
With attitude bold?
Or leave all
Your stories,
Unlived,
And untold?

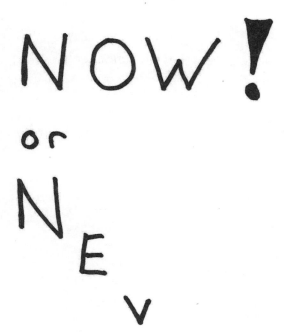

NOW!
or
NEVER?

## IF YOU MISS

If you miss
The moment when
That inspiration comes;
Chance are
You'll never get
To beat
Achievement drums!

## HIDDEN DESTINY

There is
A hidden destiny,
For each and every one;
Though finding this
Is hit and miss,
And may be never done.

Human life
Is measured by
Its length, and what is done;
But quality's
The treasure,
Not the riches nor the fun.

The easy path
Is obvious, and
Happens come what may;
It may be long,
Without a song,
Or short and fast and grey.

And quality
Relies upon
Desire to go beyond;
To probe below
The surface,
Of reflections on the pond.

Both ways
Lead to learning,
Every soul is sure of that;
But quality,
And quantity,
Will range from rich to flat.

If your path
Is stony, steep,
And winding twixt the thorns;
Just think how
You'll appreciate
The green and sculpted lawns.

So why is
This conundrum
Camouflaged in such a way?
Some may find,
If so inclined,
And some may never play.

Ego centred
Living is
At best a sole delight;
Missing all
The joys that
Loving others can excite.

So make your
Life inclusive,
Sharing out what comes your way;
Seeing how,
With smiling brow,
Contentment fills your day.


Listen to
The voices, which
Incline you how to be;
Heed your
Gut reactions,
Guiding where you cannot see.


And how much,
As a person,
Have you grown by all of this?
Would you trade
All you have made
For just one loving kiss?


If you find
That destiny
Reserved for you alone;
Welcome it,
With open arms,
See how much you've grown.

## DANGER IN THE MANGER

The danger,
In the manger,
Is the infant
Left to grow;
Without the rules
Of right and wrong,
Which they
Will need to know.

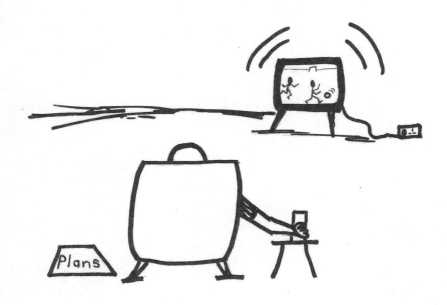

## MIGHTY MIGHTERDON

Behold the Mighty Mighterdon,
Who lives life on the edge,
Of could do this,
And might do that,
His sign the broken pledge.


The Mighterdon has
Lots of friends,
He talks with them for hours;
Of how to bake a maybe cake,
From half-baked groanstound flours.


Behold the Mighty Mighterdon,
He might get there one day;
Perhaps he will,
He might do still,
Before his hair goes grey.


The Mighterdon has
Lots of plans,
Of things he wants to do;
He has the mental energy,
But not much carry through.


Behold the Mighty Mighterdon,
Please don't stand in his way;
He's going to start,
It's in his heart,
But maybe not today!

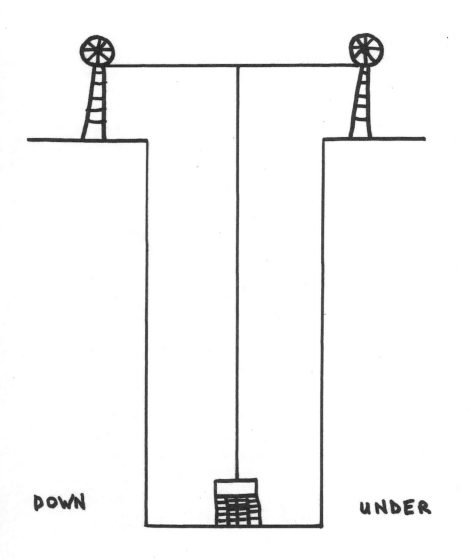

DOWN        UNDER

## WHEN DOWN THE PIT....

There's times in our lives
When try as we may,
Our overall mood
Is really quite grey.

The only way's upwards,
And things will improve;
If we make the effort,
To make the first move.

We struggle, we grapple,
To lift ourselves up;;
But despite all the effort,
Half empty our cup.

So don't see the bad times
As something to fear;
They should make us focus
On what we hold dear.

We may never know what's
The reason for this;
We feel disconnected,
There's something amiss.

Our life is so simple,
When we learn to let go;
Stop wanting and worrying
And living a show.

Whenever these times come
We shouldn't give in;
Occasional down times
Are never a sin.

Just cherish our assets,
Whatever they are;
Remember, to someone,
We may be a star.

When down in the pit,
With our chin on the floor;
We can't go no lower,
And that is for sure.

If we have a good friend
If we have our health,
We don't need possessions,
We don't need great wealth.

And if we're surrounded
With stuff soft and smelly,
We'd better be sure
To get up off our belly.

If there is one person
With whom we share love;
We are a good human,
We're loved from above.

7 x 7 + 7

# COMPENSATION AND RETRIBUTION

# FOR GOOD AND EVIL DEEDS ON EARTH

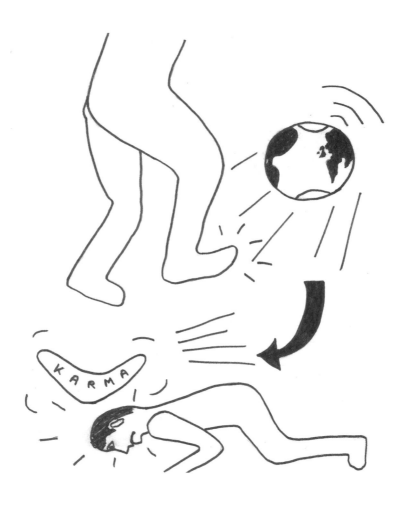

**RIPPLES**

The ripples from
The stones I throw,
On this vast,
Eternal pond;
Reach out
Into the universe,
And maybe
Far beyond.

And so it is
With things I say,
Or thoughts
That cross my mind;
Long after I have
Gone my way,
These things
Are left behind.

And even if
It were not so,
I should still
Be aware;
My deeds
Have repercussions,
Sometimes quite unfair.

And so as
I sit idly,
With these pebbles
In my hand
I gaze upon
The waters,
While on shore
I safely stand

I need to know
The vastness
Of the things
I cannot see;
The things I deem
So far away,
They are not
Part of me.

And yet we're
All connected,
Like the rivers
Of the Tao;
The future,
And the past times,
And the present,
Here and now.

And if there is
A schism,
It exists
Just in my mind;
So I had best
Be loving and
Compassionate and kind.

And cast my pebbles
Carefully,
With all this
Born in mind;
So others don't
Get drownded
By the waves
I leave behind.

## THE MEMORIES...

The memories
Of this and that
Are what you take away;
Of how you laughed
And how you cried,
And times you had in play.

The colours, smells
And tastes you knew,
In memory retained;
Of what you loved,
And what you lost,
And was your honour stained?

Who you touched
And who touched you,
And was it done for self?
Or did you share
With other souls,
Ignoring thoughts of wealth?

So seek you out
The memories
That you will take away;
Will you be worth
Your time on Earth,
Upon that Judgement Day?

## SEEING THE LIGHT

Let's invite
God here tonight,
He sure invited us!
And if He really
Did turn up,
I know we'd make a fuss!

Reach with love
To Heaven above
And send the invitation;
And if His minders
Say OK,
We'll give Him top citation.

At table head
We'll lay a spread,
Fit for our great Creator;
We'll give our best,
Meat and two veg,
And fluffy mashed potata.

We'll give a toast,
As perfect host,
In after dinner speeches;
We'll give Him thanks
For life on Earth,
Whilst eating sliced tin peaches.

We hope that He
Will smile and see
Our earnest supplication;
And not the way
We cheat and kill,
In every land and nation.

We hope His eyes
Won't see our lies,
And how we've wrecked the Earth;
How self has filled
Our troubled minds
With how much we are worth.

If He's impressed
We might be blessed,
He might just let us stay;
We're not all bad,
Just looks that way -
There's some that even pray!

We'll kneel and plead
And intercede
To our great Lord above;
And He will smile
And say to us
"All that I seek is love."

## THE HARDEST THINGS

The hardest things
We go through,
Are the things
We often hide;
Pushing down
The memories
To somewhere
Deep inside.

We gather
Bits and pieces,
Of these things
Which cut us deep;
Storing them
In shadows,
Where our darkest
Lurgies creep.

So often
Unrelated,
And undated
In our mind;
These things
Will come together,
When the
Linkages we find.

And though we
Do not like them,
'Cos our pain
They make us feel;
They're part
Of the experience,
Which makes
Our lives more real.

If life were
Full of sweet things,
With no contrast
To compare;
Just how would
We then measure
All the treasure
In our care?

It's knowing
Of the bad things,
Keeps our balance,
Makes us whole;
Defining
All our good health,
Through the
War wounds of our soul.

But if we
Build a wall around
The things
Which hurt us most;
We may never
Exorcise
That painful
Lessons ghost.

So better yet
We free them,
Let them surface
When they will;
Flotsam on
The cup of life,
Unwanted
Overspill.

The hard wounds
Cut us deeper,
Slow us down
And make us think;
A full view of
The precipice,
While standing
On the brink.

The hard stuff
Shows the difference,
Twixt the sweetness
And the sour;
Living by the
Minute,
And on good days,
By the hour.

So don't reject
The short straw,
When it seems
To be your turn;
'Cos getting through
The gritty bits
Is how you
Get to learn.

And hard can
Bring forth wisdom,
And the counsel
Of the tough;
So take the
Opportunity
To enjoy
A bit of rough.

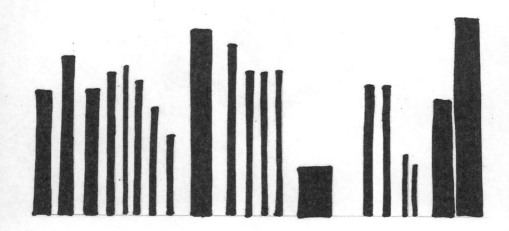

## SPIRITUAL BARCODE

Your life has a barcode,
Recording its course;
Your plans and adventures,
Your times of remorse.

Each bar is a measure,
Of highlight and low;
Of what brought you learning,
And what made you grow.

The number's a measure
Of just how you did
Did you hold tight to corners?
Or live in a skid?

Narrow bars reflecting
Where learning was thin;
The fat ones where you had
To cram it all in.

The depth of the shade
Shows how much you felt;
The black for the hard times,
Where you tightened your belt.

The spaces will show times
Where chances you missed;
That hand stretched towards you,
Those lips left unkissed.

That smile left unsmiled,
And those kind words unspoke;
The laughter unlaughed,
At the kindly meant joke.

The length of the code
Shows your span here on Earth;
With length on its own
Not a measure of worth.

With learning and loving
The best to take back;
Hope there's no white ones,
And sure, lots of black.

The codes are encrypted
In heart, mind and soul;
Though how they're awarded,
Beyond your control.

Sincere in your witness,
Your thought, word and deed;
With no points awarded
For ego and greed.

So think of your scanner,
As through life you pass;
Think how you will show up
On God's scanner glass.

Will you be marked up
As "quality gain"?
Or put in "recycling",
To come back again?

For God has the measure
Of all souls that live;
He gave you your spark,
So your life you could live.

So take him back something
Of which you are proud;
Something which makes you
Stand out from the crowd.

A barcode not filled up
With treasure and pride;
But one that shows how you
Both loved and you tried.

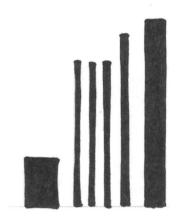

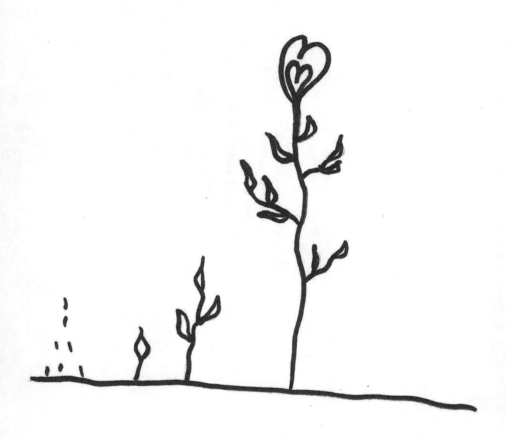

## IN THE SEEDS ....

In the seeds
Of here and now
The future
Has its roots;
How well we water,
Tend and care
Affects
The strength of shoots.

If we tend
With hands of love,
And water
With our tears,
And mulch around
With lessons learned,
The growth
Will spread for years.

The sunshine of
Our joyfulness
Will strengthen
Root and stem;
And give a firm
Foundation for
The likes of
Us and them.

So hark to
Heartfelt messages,
Which wisdom
Brings to mind;
And know that if
You truly seek,
You're sure
To truly find.

And for the future,
Let it not
Be left
To run to chance;
Let's motivate,
And cultivate,
And orchestrate
The dance.

And should we
Be uncertain
Of the best way
To proceed;
We only need
Ask Spirit and
They're sure
To give us heed.

So let us sing
And laugh
And play
And seek the inspiration;
And Spirit will
Articulate
Our future
Path creation.

So as the seeds
Of here and now
Lay dormant
In our hand,
Let's be so careful
What we do,
Let loving
Be what's planned.

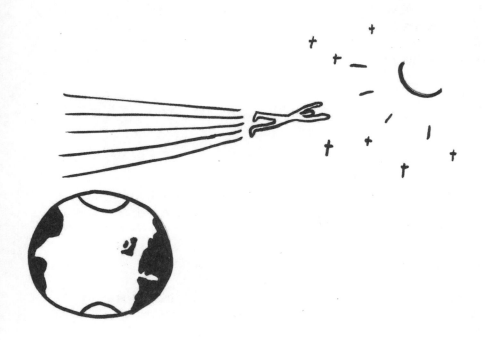

## REFLECTIONS

Will you leave
A vapour trail,
In the night sky
Of your life?
Emblazoned there
In glory?
Or dispersed
In clouds of strife?

Will you shake
The hands of friends,
Whose lives
You have enriched?
Will you count
The poor man there,
Whose ragged clothes
You stitched?

Will your good deeds
Vaunt themselves,
Where others
They have failed?
Or will you
On the spikes
Of others' mischief
Be impaled?

Will you raise
A glass of cheer,
And toast
Those happy times?
Or wonder why
You missed that chance,
When they play
Your exit chimes?

Will your face
Have laughter lines?
And your eyes
A glint of glee?
Or will you pass
Frustrated,
With a harsh
Unspoken plea?

Now's the time
To think it through,
And change
The way you are!
A little bit
Of effort
And you can be
A Spirit star!

7 x 7 + 7

# OTHER BITS

## UMBOLO KUMOLO

Umbolo Kumolo
Awakes with a yawn
His half open eyes
See the African dawn.
He's tall
And he's wiry,
His body is lean;
There's many
A drought year
Umbolo has seen.

The shimmering grasslands
Stretch out
Far and near;
Umbolo surveys them
His hand on his spear;
He walks with a rhythm,
A long loping stride;
His ebony features
And heart
Filled with pride.

The harsh dusty landscape
Is hard to survive;
Umbolo is grateful
That he's still alive;
No shoes has he worn
Since the time
Of his birth;
His feet know the blessing
Of sweet
Mother Earth.

Umbolo runs quickly,
Umbolo runs fleet,
His spear helps him capture
The food he must eat;
He kills
Not for pleasure,
And seeks out
No rival,
His life being focussed
On daily survival.

The dust fills his lungs
And the heat saps his strength;
But he shows no weakness
His strides even length;
He moves
Smooth and quickly,
This noble Masai,
Living life
As it happens,
He never asks why.

His pace is quite even,
His stride covers much;
There's strength
And there's gentleness,
Both in his touch;
He gathers to eat
And he gathers to wear;
No need for
Possessions,
Abundance to spare.

He travels quite fast
When the day's
First begun;
Seeking the shade
In the hot midday sun;
He's always alert
For the dangers around,
His eyes peeled
For movement,
His ears tuned for sound.

He'll fight if he has to,
But seeks out no foe;
And those who
Would mock him,
Best not let it show;
For if he is challenged
There'll be
No half - measure;
He'll fight like a lion,
His life is his treasure.

He needs no companion,
Complete on his own,
His life skills
Were perfect
Before he'd full grown;
Respecting all wildlife,
He learns from their ways;
He's studied
Their moves
With his warrior gaze.

Umbolo lives solo
For most of his life;
But if fancy takes him
He'll find him a wife;
Complete though
He may be,
When all's said and done,
His instinct,
A bloodline
Assured through a son.

Umbolo Kumolo
Lies down with a yawn,
His eyes watch the sunset
With no sign of scorn;
He curls up,
Relaxing,
No fear
And no pain;
Umbolo Kumolo
On the African plain.

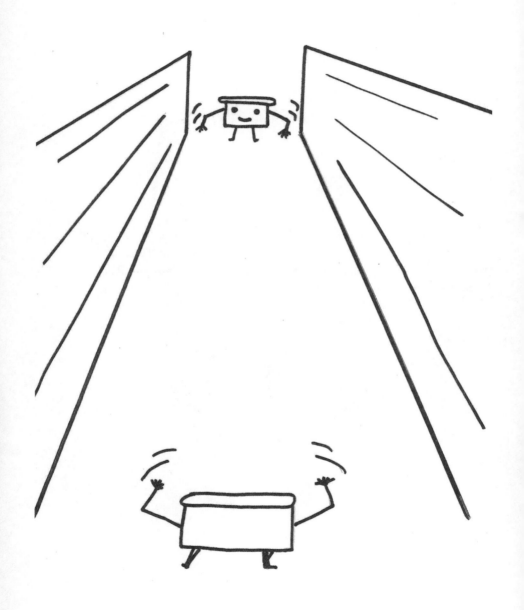

## THE DUAL

The aisles were quite empty,
At midnight plus four;
When two tubs of yellow
Jumped down on the floor.

Each took position,
One at each aisle end;
The dual of the spreadables,
To be fought to the end.

The bread and the cutlery,
Both stood close by;
With great expectation,
And surfaces dry.

Senora the Flora
Was quick to take aim;
With half price reduction
Her main claim to fame.

The butter did splutter,
And nearly did skid;
But threw out an anchor,
She kept carefully hid.

Flora pressed on with
Attack unabated;
Shouted with relish,
"I'm polyunsaturated!"

Unimpressed butter
Looked quite presidential;
"Blow your airs and graces,
My fats are essential!"

Then Flora, low fat,
Threw in low cholesterol;
"Straight from the fridge,
I spread on the freshest roll!"

Butter smiled knowingly
Said "you fatless freak!
Anything less and
Your wrapper would creak!"

"My flavour is sunshine,
Green grass and fresh air;
Made from the best milk,
My bits are all there!"

Flora senora
Said "I'm fresh and pure;
No chance of weight gain,
I'm better I'm sure!"

Butter responded well,
All pat and taped;
"I may come from cows,
But I'm not oil seed raped!"

The Flora, though reeling,
Was quick to shout back
"You go off so quickly,
You rancid grease pack!"

The butter smiled sweetly,
But had speed in recoil
"Turn up the heat dear,
You're nothing but oil!"

The bread and the cutlery
Jumped in the fray
They set about spreading
Til tubs empty lay!

And all that was left
As a sign of the war,
Was two yellow streaks,
In the dust on the floor!

## NUTKO VERUTKO

Nutko Verutko
Was perfectly mad!
Always laughing
And giggling,
He didn't do sad!

His madness
Was catching,
The sort people liked;
You'd think
He'd been drinking,
And drinks
Had been spiked!

His laughter
Infectious,
His eyes full of glee!
If that, friends,
Is madness...
I want some
For me!!

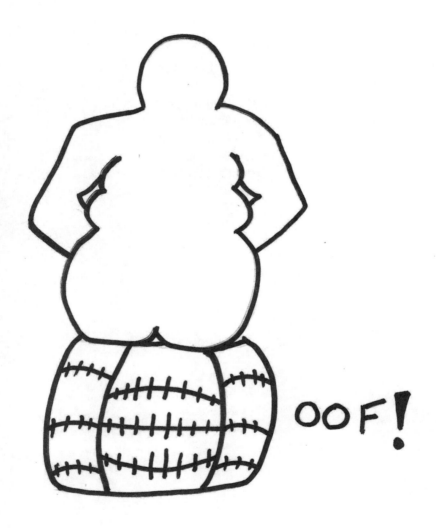

## OOF SAID THE POOF

Oof said the poof,
Someone's sitting on me;
A really big bottom,
And I cannot see!

There I was waiting,
All fluffy and free;
When this really big bottom
Descended on me!

I've tried looking this way,
I've tried looking that;
But I can't see nuffin,
This bottom's so fat!

I'm not such a posh poof,
I'm normal and square;
Being squashed by this bottom
Is really not fair!

I know it's my role,
Providing a seat;
But can the next bottom
Be somewhat more neat!!

## IT'S WET AND WINDY....

It's wet and windy
In Rawlpindhi,
The rain is lashing down;
The Oscatar of Otakar
Is dancing
With a clown.

The sole recluse
Of Syracuse
Lives Tuesday's in a tower;
The rest of the week,
He's up the creek
Pretending he's a flower.

The Mighty Vann,
Of Raglapahn
Thinks cleanliness is power;
He takes a bath
10 times a week,
And every day a shower.

The Diddley Dum
Is scratching his bum,
And wiggling both his ears;
He stands on his head
At the foot of the bed,
He's done it now for years.

The Wangle Fan Dan
Of Agerican
Keeps all his shoes in a bag;
He's got a dog with no legs,
That he props up on pegs,
Which at night he takes for a drag.

The Marshioness
Of Dungeoness
Is really rather rude;
She swims by the stars
And drives fast cars
And dances around in the nude.

The Bandoozelly Dott
Of Piddley Pott
Spends all of his money on stickers;
He'll stick them on carrots,
And short legged parrots,
And some on his wife's frilly knickers.

If you want to be friends,
It rather depends
Upon your level of vanity;
They've got no flare,
They're inclined to stare,
And you might just lose your sanity.

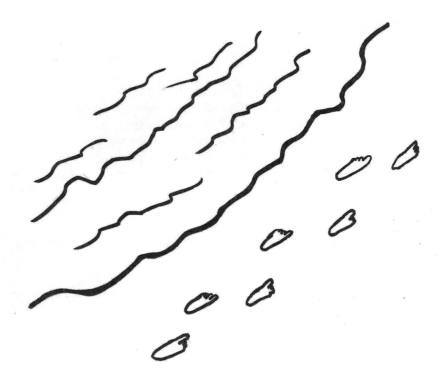

## FOOTPRINTS IN THE SAND

The sand it shows
The footprints,
Of where my feet
Have trod,
The footprints
Of a human,
Quietly in search
Of God.
In silent contemplation
Of the wonders
Of the sea;
A walking meditation,
Of the lifeforce
Known as me.
The glittering of sunlight
As the waters
Ebb and flow,
With patterns,
Always changing,
And a gentle orange glow.
The fluffy, leading edges,
Of the calmly
Lapping surf,
Reaching to
Caress these feet,
Which walk upon the Earth.
And as the waters
Touch upon
The patterns in the sand,
All traces go,
There's none to show,
As if that's what was planned.

## PERCILLUS BERILLUS.....

Percillus Berillus,
The gay legionnaire,
Had white leather pop socks,
And bright orange hair!

His helmet had sequins,
(The one on his head)
And his shield had a picture
Of fun times in bed!

His skill with the short sword
Was known far and near,
And he never missed
When he pushed forth his spear!

He used his right hand
For javelin pitching;
The left one he saved
For where he was itching!

A fiend with the crossbow,
His bolt an impresser,
On Fridays and Sundays
He was a cross - dresser!

Like all Roman soldiers,
He liked to close ranks;
Percillus behind you
Would never shoot blanks!

The stories about him
Would terrify regions;
His prowess was known
Throughout all Roman legions!

They tried him in chariots,
But took other courses;
He couldn't concentrate
When placed behind horses!

His name was a legend
When building a ramp;
He was known for his leaning,
This Roman so camp!

A man to have with you
On every campaign;
With him in the back row,
Advances soon came!

He plunged into battle,
He'd never been beat;
He liked to press hard
With his foe in retreat!

He loved all those straight roads
Made by engineers;
His best friends among them
Had been bent for years!

He'd been on the galleys,
And rowed with the best;
At each port they called at
His oar didn't rest!

He'd fought with the British,
And conquered the Gauls;
He was known for his valour,
His strength and his balls!

He fought the unruly,
Subdued every nation;
He fought at his best
In a circle formation!

Percillus Berillus,
A true Roman name;
Always up at the front,
But behind when he came!

**About Ray Edwards**......................

Growing up in London in the early 1950's my earliest recollections were coloured by memories of a life much quieter and calmer than seems possible now. World War 2 was not long over; people of other nationalities were a rarity; buses and trains would get you anywhere, the radio was the main national entertainment (I had a home made crystal set on the shelf over my bed); people read books for pleasure and talked to each other with a genuine desire to connect; politicians were honourable people with a sense of responsibility and service; there was hope for what the future would bring and respect and fairness were predominant in joined up communities which took care to look after and look out for each other and their own families. Large numbers of people still went to church and Sunday School was the norm for young children. Church fayres and jumble sales were packed with people, and there was never much left afterwards.

Television (when it did arrive) was in small 9 inch screens and black and white only. There were no daytime programmes, no commercial channels, and no TV at all on Sunday nights after 6pm! Skiffle and jazz were the daring new music of the pre rock and roll era. Family Favourites, Children's Hour, the Goon Show, the Navy Lark, Beyond our Ken, Listen with Mother, Workers Playtime and Forces Favourites were listened to avidly. There were relatively few motor cars (and no motorways), even fewer households with a phone (mobile phones had not been invented), there were two post deliveries per day – regularly – and policemen were there to protect the law abiding and not the human rights of those arrested! Winning the Football Pools was everyone's dream of making a fortune (and everyone supported a team somewhere). England did indeed seem a very green and pleasant land!

I read a wide variety of books (often under my bedclothes at night, when I should have been going to sleep) ranging from science fiction (which is exactly what it was then – I remember the first sputnik being launched by the Russians), historical accounts of Roman, Greek and English battles and campaigns, the Famous Five and Secret Seven, boys adventure stories, Billy Bunter, and the Adventures of The Saint.

I was introduced to the wonders of the art world with my father being artistic and collecting a series of books about the great masters - full of wonderful colour pictures (I remember liking Reubens because he used a lot of red paint, Salvador Dali whose pictures were busy and outrageous, and Picasso who appeared as if he liked a drink from the way he painted people). Many books then were still black and white only, but the colour was added by the reader's imagination. On the family bookshelf there was also a poetry book called The Golden Treasury, which I looked at occasionally and understood very little of – I seem to recall liking verses by Rudyard Kipling.

At school I was quite good at reading and spelling, but got progressively lazy as I my school career reached its latter years. I moved up to Solihull when I was 11 years old, and really felt as if my roots had been cut. My only sister stayed in London when we moved, and home life was never quite the same again.

My first real interest in writing poetry seemed to be ignited during family stays on a farm in Derbyshire during the autumn school half term holidays, and then only the odd verse here and there. I have included two of those verses in this first book to show those first inspirations. It was not until I became involved with the spiritualist church and went on a course in Cober Hill in Yorkshire in 2006 that things really began to happen. It was then that my meditations began to produce inspired verse in significant quantity – and so I was hooked!

7 x 7 + 7